GALATIANS

GALATIANS
VERSE-BY-VERSE GRAPHIC NOVEL WEB TRANSLATION

ILLUSTRATIONS BY THOMAS FASANO

**1 & 2 GALATIANS: VERSE-BY-VERSE GRAPHIC NOVEL
WEB TRANSLATION**

Illustrations Copyright © 2025 by Thomas Fasano

The World English Bible is in the public domain.

Published by Coyote Canyon Press
Claremont, California

ISBN: 979-8-9937072-2-8

1:1 – PAUL, AN APOSTLE (NOT FROM MEN, NEITHER THROUGH MAN, BUT THROUGH JESUS CHRIST, AND GOD THE FATHER, WHO RAISED HIM FROM THE DEAD),

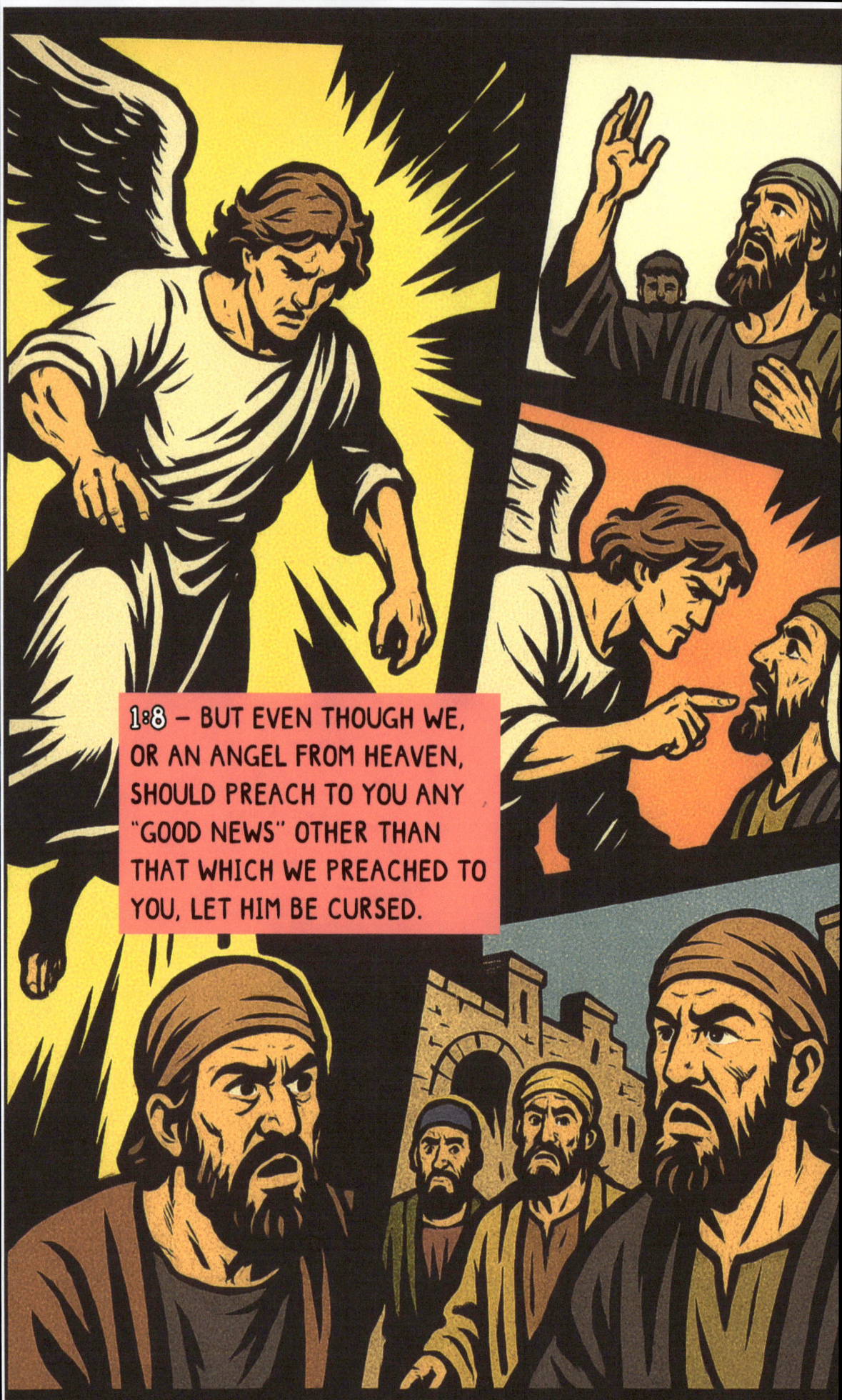

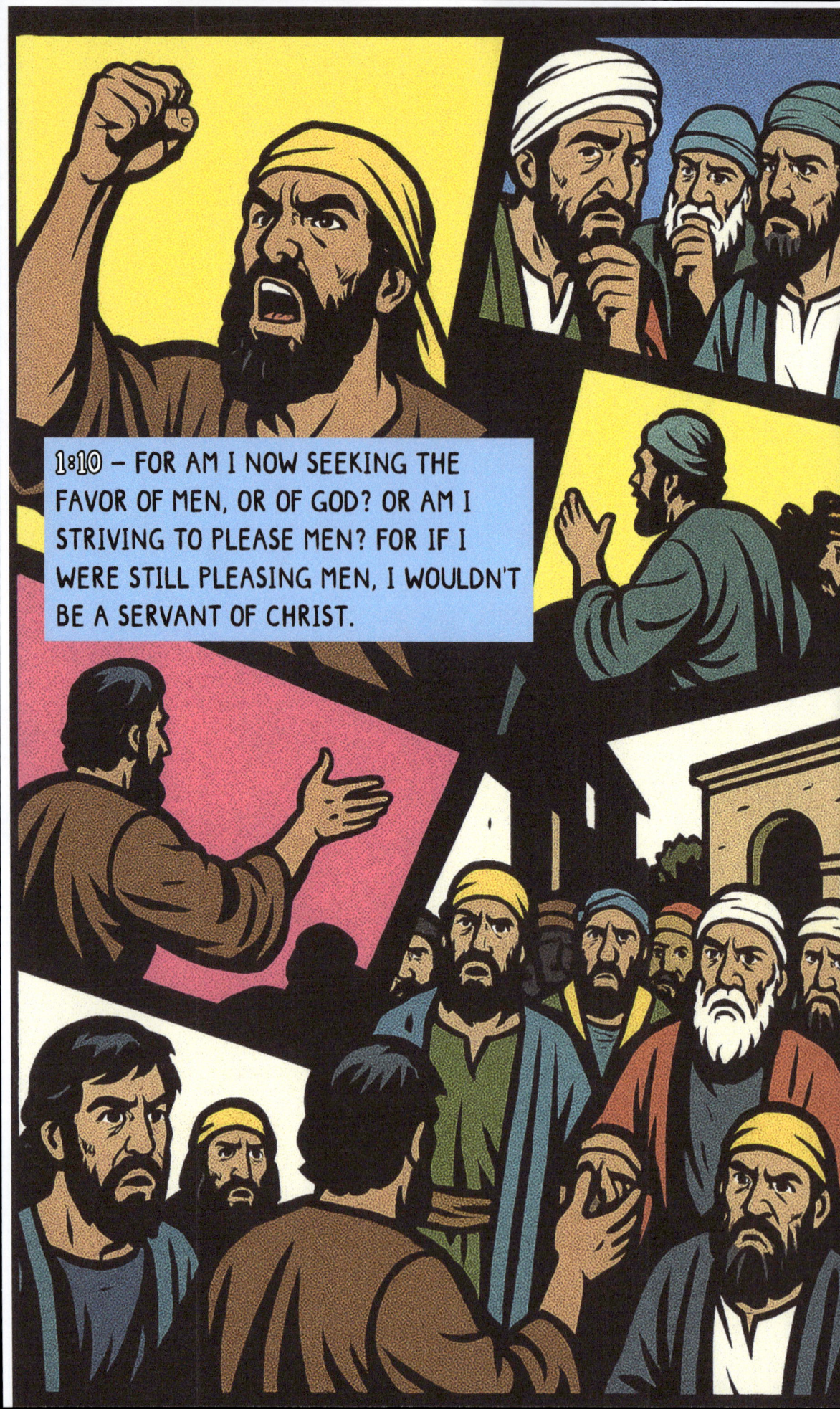

1:19 – BUT OF THE OTHER APOSTLES I SAW NO ONE, EXCEPT JAMES, THE LORD'S BROTHER.

1:20 – NOW ABOUT THE THINGS WHICH I WRITE TO YOU, BEHOLD, BEFORE GOD, I'M NOT LYING.

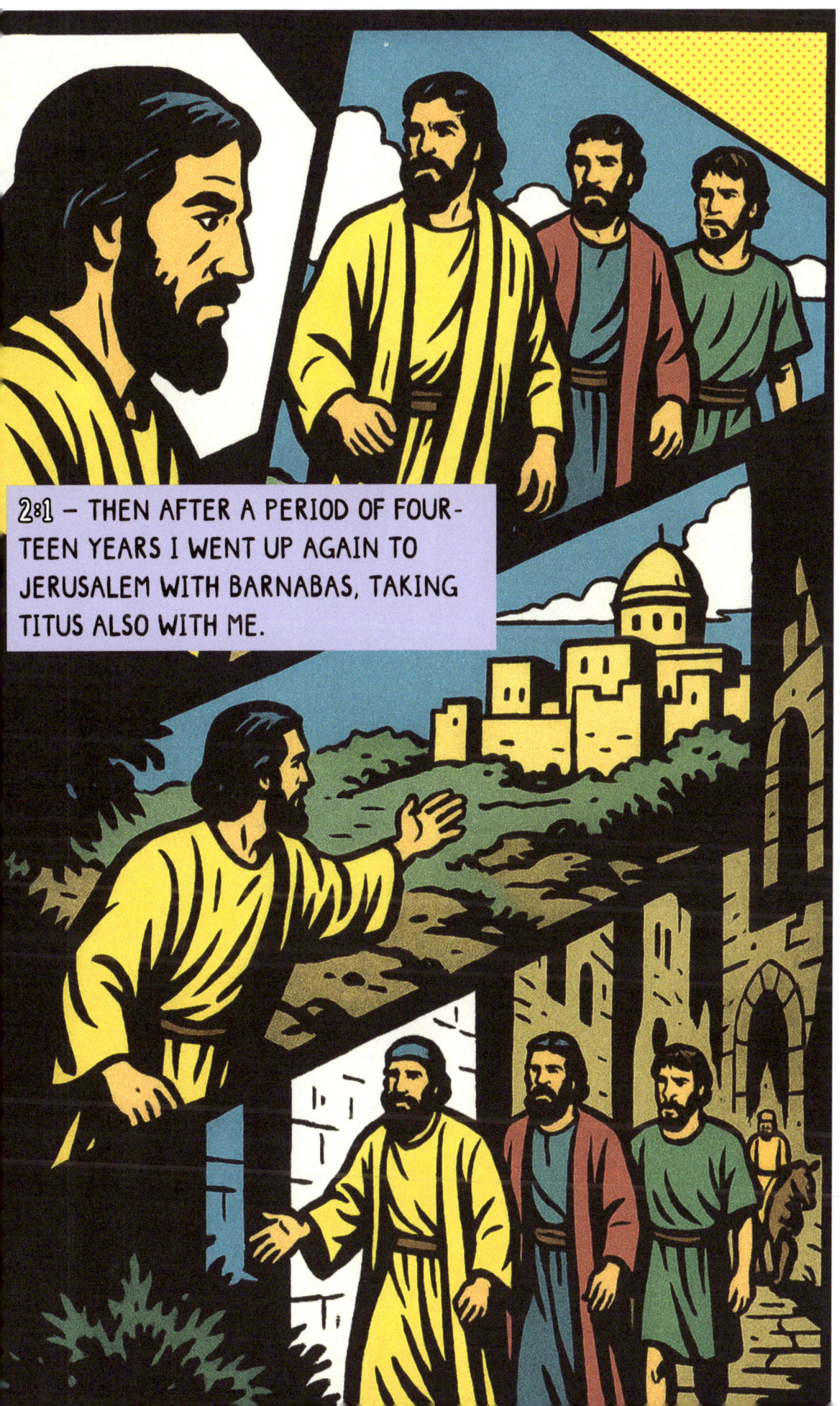

2:5 – TO WHOM WE GAVE NO PLACE IN THE WAY OF SUBJECTION, NOT FOR AN HOUR, THAT THE TRUTH OF THE GOOD NEWS MIGHT CONTINUE WITH YOU.

2:9 – AND WHEN THEY PERCEIVED THE GRACE THAT WAS GIVEN TO ME, JAMES AND CEPHAS AND JOHN, THEY WHO WERE REPUTED TO BE PILLARS, GAVE TO ME AND BARNABAS THE RIGHT HAND OF FELLOWSHIP, THAT WE SHOULD GO TO THE GENTILES, AND THEY TO THE CIRCUMCISION.

2:13 – AND THE REST OF THE JEWS JOINED HIM IN HIS HYPOCRISY; SO THAT EVEN BARNABAS WAS CARRIED AWAY WITH THEIR HYPOCRISY.

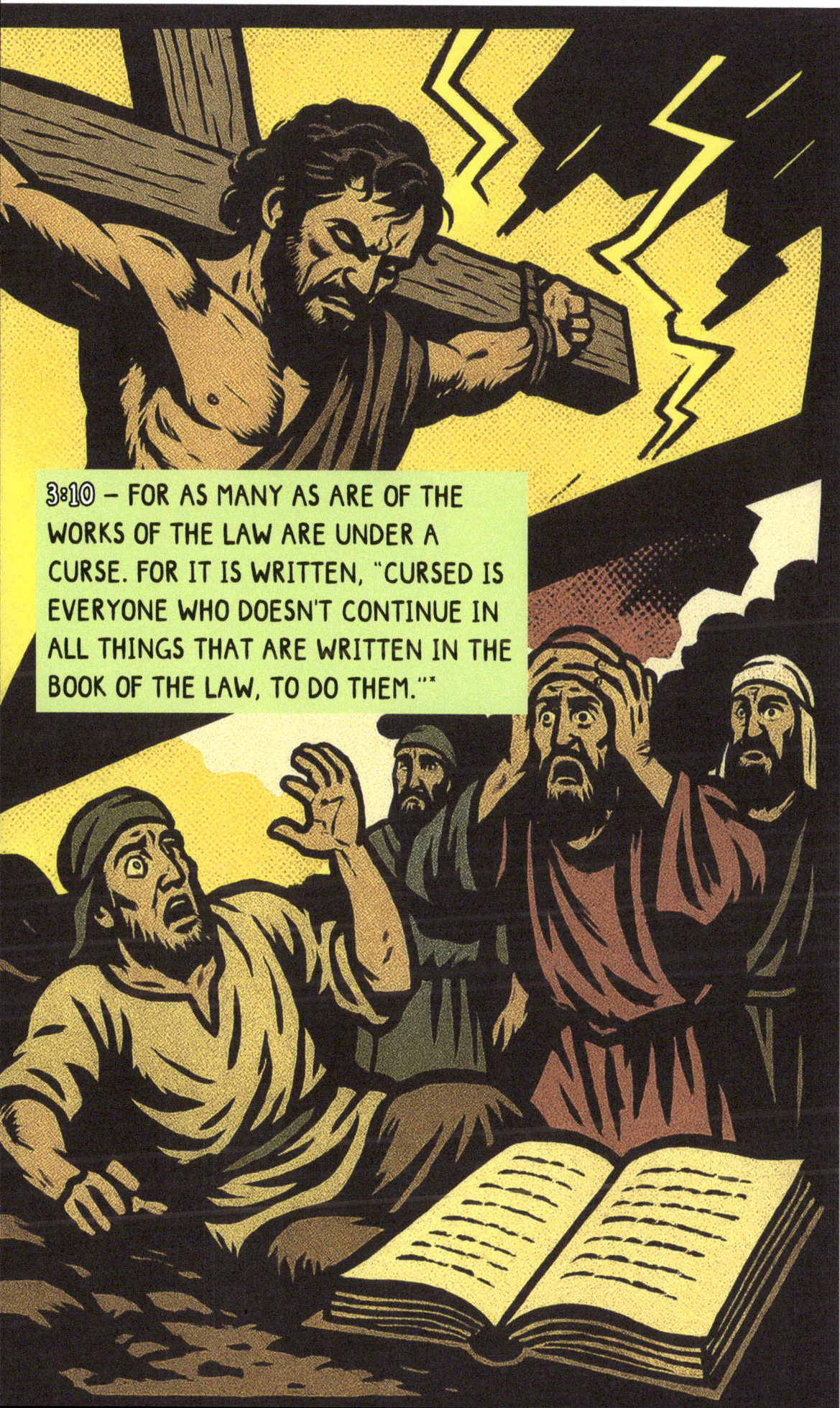

3:16 – NOW THE PROMISES WERE SPOKEN TO ABRAHAM AND TO HIS SEED. HE DOESN'T SAY, "TO SEEDS," AS OF MANY, BUT AS OF ONE, "TO YOUR SEED,"* WHICH IS CHRIST.

4:3 – SO WE ALSO, WHEN WE WERE CHILDREN, WERE HELD IN BONDAGE UNDER THE ELEMENTAL PRINCIPLES OF THE WORLD.

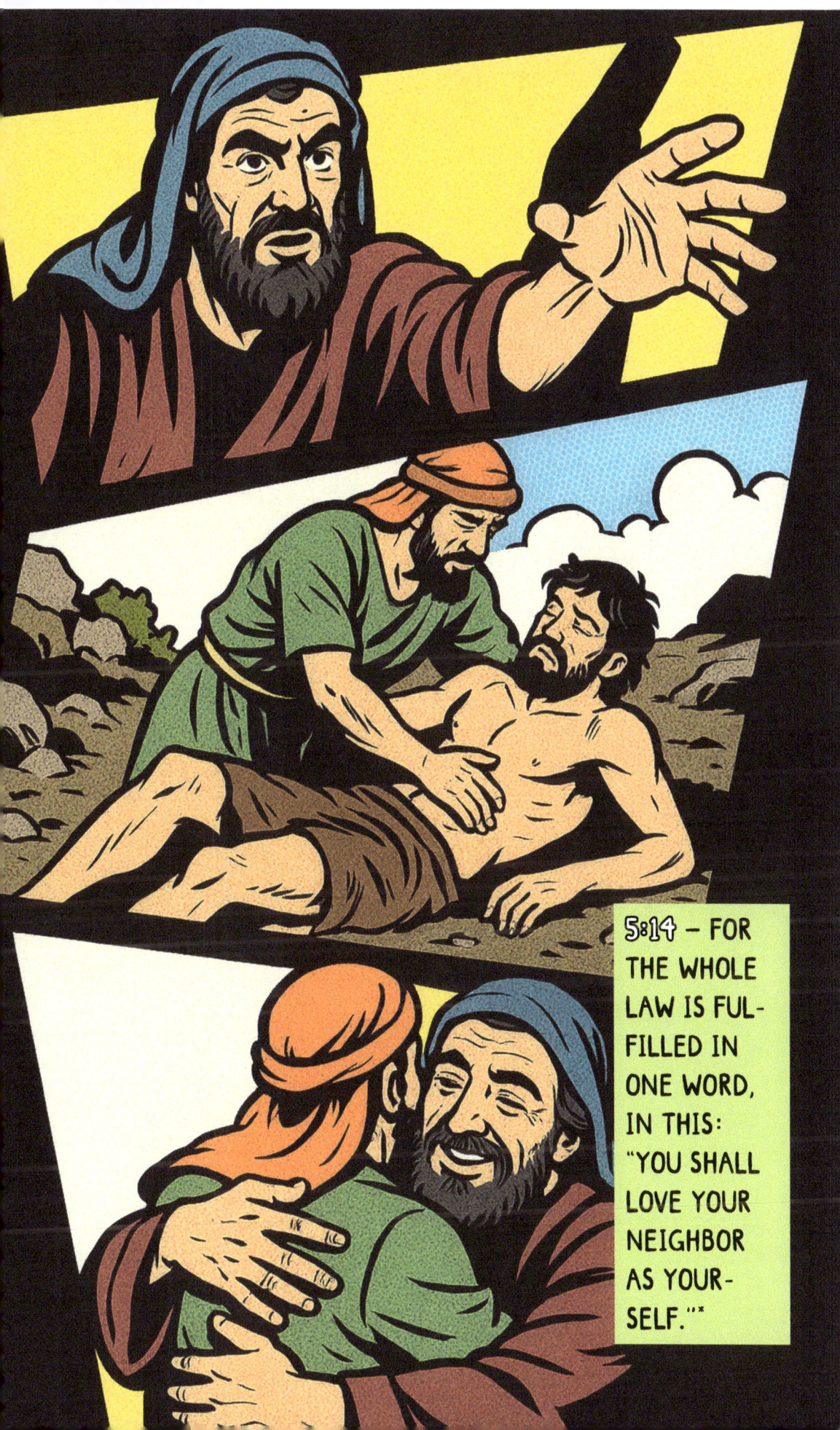

6:6 – BUT LET HIM WHO IS TAUGHT IN THE WORD SHARE ALL GOOD THINGS WITH HIM WHO TEACHES.

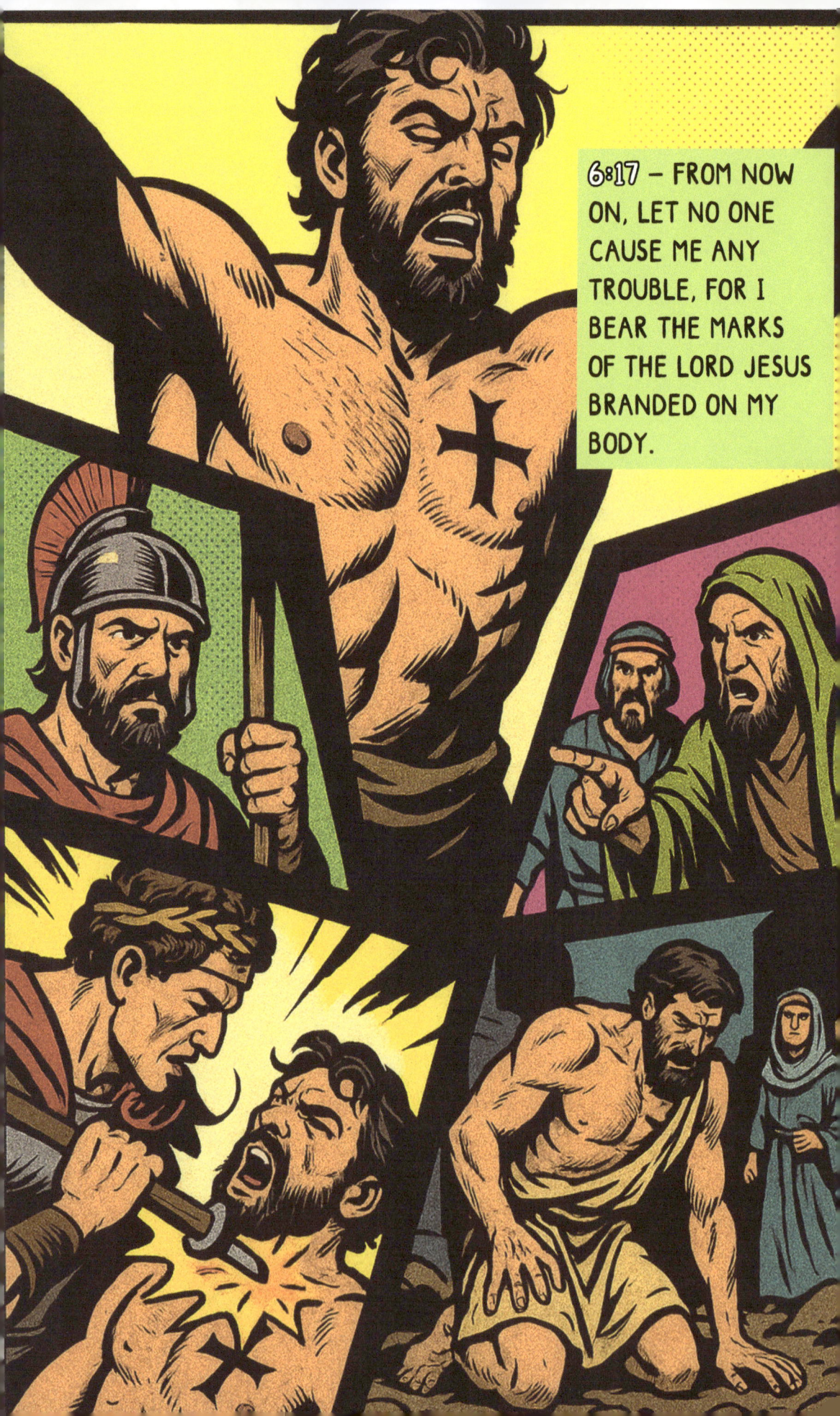

www.ingramcontent.com/pod-product-compliance
Lightning Source LLC
Chambersburg PA
CBHW060937170426
43194CB00027B/2977